Twitter

How To Market & Make Money With Twitter

By Ace McCloud
Copyright © 2014

Disclaimer

The information provided in this book is designed to provide helpful information on the subjects discussed. This book is not meant to be used, nor should it be used, to diagnose or treat any medical condition. For diagnosis or treatment of any medical problem, consult your own physician. The publisher and author are not responsible for any specific health or allergy needs that may require medical supervision and are not liable for any damages or negative consequences from any treatment, action, application or preparation, to any person reading or following the information in this book. Any references included are provided for informational purposes only. Readers should be aware that any websites or links listed in this book may change.

Table of Contents

Introduction

Chapter 1: Optimizing Your Twitter Account So That People Want To Follow You

Chapter 2: How To Successfully Manage Your Twitter Account

Chapter 3: Marketing And Making Money On Twitter

Chapter 4: Putting It All Together In An Action Plan For Success

Chapter 5: The Best Twitter Resources

Conclusion

Preview Of "Money: The Top 100 Best Ways To Make And Manage Money"

Check Out My Other Books

DEDICATED TO THOSE WHO ARE PLAYING THE GAME OF LIFE TO

WIN

KEEP ON PUSHING AND NEVER GIVE UP!

Ace McCloud

Special Bonus: If you would like to get my latest **E-Books for FREE** just **CLICK HERE**

Introduction

I want to thank you and congratulate you for downloading the book: "Twitter: How To Market and Make Money With Twitter."

Twitter is a very powerful, top-rated social media website with over 200 million users. Twitter is best known for its 140 character "tweets," which people use to communicate news, information, and opinions. The messages are short and to the point. Twitter is one of the most well-known social media networks and has been gaining popularity as each year goes by. The name Twitter literally means "a short burst of information," as well as "chirps from birds." Hence, Twitter is a microblogging website with a bird as its main theme. Many celebrities and famous figures have Twitter accounts, along with many other influential people.

While some people see Twitter as "just another social media website," the truth is that Twitter is a powerful communication tool, especially when used in the right ways. Many major companies such as Dell, Starbucks, JetBlue, Comcast, The Home Depot, Southwestern Airlines, H&R Block and Ford Motor Company all have active Twitter accounts—Starbucks even operates multiple accounts! Twitter has many benefits that make it perfect for marketing and making money.

There are many social media platforms out there for you to market and make money on, so why pick Twitter? First and foremost, Twitter has an insanely low learning curve—anybody can make an account within seconds and start tweeting. Your account has the ability to be automated, which means that you don't even have to be in front of your computer to work magic. Many key influencers use Twitter and have verified accounts, so if you are trying to break into a field, you can use Twitter to potentially connect with them.

One unique thing about Twitter is that you can use third-party programs and software to really get the most out of it—you can easily pull data from your page as well as the pages of others to build an audience. You can also analyze the location of your audience, and pull out other types of useful data. Finally, Twitter is best known for its use of hashtags, which are searchable keywords that can help you narrow your market and directly connect to your core audience. If you are a person who is looking to market your products, make money and spend your attention on your business rather than on your marketing efforts, then look no further, because Twitter is the place you want to be!

There are so many more benefits to using Twitter, especially once you've built a solid audience. You can use Twitter to keep your customers updated on your company, hand out coupons, handle customer complaints, react to feedback, promote blogs, give out free material and most importantly, build rapport with your audience. Twitter is available in many forms—you can use it in your web browser on a Mac or Windows PC or you can download the Twitter app to your smart-phone or tablet and take it on the go. In today's day in age, many people are connected no matter where they go.

To utilize all these great benefits, you must first become a master at using Twitter. There is much more beyond filling out your profile, sending a few tweets, and then hoping that you invoke a response. This book contains proven steps and strategies on how to unlock the secrets of Twitter and create a master strategy so that you can jump right to the top. In this book, you will learn how to create a killer following base with the potential to reach up to 100,000+ users. You will also learn how to optimize your profile, make the most of your twitter page and create engaging tweets so that you are constantly capturing your audience's attention and gaining more followers.

As you read on, you will discover the top strategy on how to properly and effectively market your products on Twitter as well as many other ways to make some extra money. At the end, you will find a step-by-step plan that puts it all together and walks you through the process of becoming a twitter pro. If you want to discover all these secrets about Twitter and more, such as the best times to tweet and what kind of tweets you should send, read on, take notes, and work your way towards becoming a Twitter master.

Thanks for downloading this book and I hope that you enjoy it!

Chapter 1: Optimizing Your Twitter Account So That People Want To Follow You

So you've got a Twitter account—great! Where do you begin? Twitter is very different than many of the traditional social media websites that exist. At first glance, it can be very confusing! However, setting up your Twitter account can be very easy and if you do it right from the start, you can set yourself up to attract thousands upon thousands of followers.

First, let's focus on your username. This is what other users can use to search for you or mention you in a post. My username is Ace McCloud@AcesEbooks. One of the best features on Twitter is that you can change your username as many times as you want—just be wary not to confuse your followers. Your username usually reflects your name, the purpose of your account, or both. For example, my username reflects my name and the fact that I am an author who writes E-books. I also publish in books as well, but my main focus is on e-books, as I love to provide easily clickable links in my books to super useful information. Your username can only be 15 characters long so take a bit of time to pick it wisely! But it really shouldn't be that hard, it should come naturally to you.

Here is a great tip that you can use to pick your username—if you're not a corporate business like Starbucks but you're not exactly a well-known figure in your industry, you can make your username creative to help you stand out. Get really creative here and use rhyming or alliteration to make it memorable. For example, if your name is Harold and you own a hibachi restaurant, your username could be HibachiHarold.

Second, let's focus on location. When you're filling your Twitter profile out there is a box where you can add your location. Many people don't take advantage of filling out their location but it can be a really powerful tool, especially if you live in a big city. The location box can really help out businesses that serve certain demographics. For example, let's say that you own a pretzel stand in New York City. Thousands of people walk the streets of New York City every day. Let's say that somebody in the city suddenly gets a craving for a nice, hot pretzel, so they turn to Twitter to find a pretzel business in New York City. If your username is something like @PretzelMania and your location is listed as New York City, you will rank high in the search results.

When it comes to filling out your location it is also important to be smart. You have to figure out *how* your audience is searching the location. For example, if you did research on New York City, you'd find out that more people are searching with the term "New York City" than "NYC." So, you'd want to list your location specifically as "New York City" and not "NYC." However the abbreviations can be very useful in a variety of other situations on twitter.

Third, let's take a look at a very, very important part of your profile: your bio. Your bio is a small box that allows you to introduce yourself to your audience. Don't overlook it! When writing out your bio, write and rewrite it. Research keywords in your field and use them in the description. Include a hashtag or two (we will get to more on hashtags later). You can even use this space for a call-to-action (CTA). If you're offering a free promotion or some other type of valuable resource, be sure to have your bio filled out, as this is one of the first things people see when checking you out. Your bio is only 160 characters, so be sure to use that space well!

Finally, let's take a look at two other very valuable spaces on your profile: your profile and header picture. These pictures will represent you and/or your brand. Visual aids are very powerful tools and your audience will be more likely to remember you through your images. For your profile image, it is best to use either a photo that depicts your brand's name or logo. If you're an individual, like an author, musician, etc, you can use a professional portrait of yourself. Your header, which is like a cover photo, is a huge space on your profile. You can use a picture that further represents your purpose or you can even use it as a space to provide your audience with more details or a CTA. You can get a professional header done very easily on the website www.fiverr.com, and it only costs five dollars. Many people include their business name on the header, a logo image, their website, or any other contact information they may want to include. A good size to specify for twitter headers is 1500 by 500.

A good tip when it comes to picking out images is to stay simple. Try to use a good color scheme and limit it to 2-3 colors that go well together. If you try to crowd your profile with pictures or colors that don't go well together, it will not be visually appealing and may actually drive your audience away.

Optimizing Your Tweets

Your tweets are the heart of your Twitter account. They are what your followers and audience will see. Your tweets are important for engaging with your audience, giving your profile a unique voice, and providing quality content.

General Structure of a Tweet

Your tweet can be about anything, but to make it effective, you can follow these guidelines. The maximum length of a tweet is 140 characters although research shows the average one is only 28-40 characters long. The research here may be onto a trend—short tweets are 180% more likely to attract interaction from your audience. A tweet is typically a call to action (meaning you want your audience to click on a link that takes them somewhere else) or a question that will prompt a direct responses from your audience. Many users on Twitter also like to tweet quotes.

There is a formula that you can follow to ensure that you are sending out effective tweets. The typical structure of an effective tweet goes as follows: content – hashtag – media. For example, if I were to send out an effective tweet, it would look something like this:

Discover the power of #Leadership! My #Ebook is #FREE today! [hyperlink to the Amazon page where users can access the ebook]. Also, be sure to shorten your links that you use on twitter using programs like bitly or google.

As you can see, I wrote my content (Discover the power of leadership. My ebook is free today) and I integrated hashtags, so if people are looking for a free leadership ebook, they will find me. Then I added the link where my audience can access my book.

It is important to use keywords in your tweets, otherwise your message will not be clear. Let's pretend that I sent out that last tweet, but instead I wrote it like this: Hey everyone I just finished my new #ebook please download it! [media]. Though I used a hashtag to signify that I am talking about an ebook, nobody would know the nature of the ebook and thus it would not attract as many interested people and probably no re-tweets.

When coming up with the keywords in your content, be sure to use powerful, attention-grabbing words. Words and phrases such as "discover," "foolproof," or "get the facts now," are great for catching one's eye and making them curious to learn more.

The Length of Your Tweets

This is very important! The optimum length of your Tweets is around 125 characters. That leaves 15 characters left over so that people can easily re-tweet you! Be sure to take this into account when making your tweets.

Change Up Your Tweets

If you are doing a large amount of Tweets, then it is essential that you mix up your tweets with different words so that you don't have any problems with twitter blocking the same tweet over and over. Just change up your tweets a little bit using slightly different words or hashtags.

The Tweeting Formula

Now that you know how to optimize your Twitter profile and how to write an effective tweet, it is time to learn the logistics. Creating an engaging tweet is just the tip of the iceberg. You know how to write an engaging tweet but now you are faced with the question of, "How can I get my followers to interact with my tweets?" Luckily, there is a great answer to this question!

The best tweeting strategy is to send out 5 tweets per day. 1/5 of those tweets should be instructional (such as a how-to video or article), 1/5 should be inspirational (like a quote), 1/5 should be fun (maybe a relevant 'fun fact' article), 1/5 should be promotional of yourself, and 1/5 should be a retweet. By doing this, you can reach a vast audience and you can keep your content interesting and engaging. You can save yourself time by setting up your account to automatically post pre-written tweets. You will learn more about this in a few chapters.

However, this method does not work for everyone. I personally like to automate my tweets ahead of time and do 1 tweet every 30 minutes 24 hours a day. My ebooks have a worldwide audience, so I go more for volume to make sure that everyone will have access to my newest free books or some of my favorite books no matter where they live and what time zone they are in. The choice of method is up to you, they both can be very effective.

Finally, it is important to strategically time your tweet. Sure, you can send out tweets during any time of the day but unless the majority of your audience is online, you may not reach them. The best way to get the most out of this strategy is to know where your followers are living. For example, if you're sending tweets from California, you want to be sure that you're timing them using the right time zone so that you're not reaching people in New Jersey.

You will also have to do a bit of your own research to figure out what times the majority of your followers are online, but there are some general time frames in which it is better to send out tweets. They are:

7am to 8am
1pm to 2pm
5pm to 6pm
9pm to 10pm

For business professionals, weekends are an especially good time to send out tweets because that is when most people have time to relax, unwind and sit down with their social media accounts. These types of people are usually very busy during the week and may not have as much time to check their Twitter accounts or interact with other users.

The Power of Hashtags

Hashtags are words or phrases that begin with a # symbol to indicate trending topics or keywords. They can actually be really powerful tools. Hashtags can be a single keyword that is related to your post or it can be the slogan of your business. For example, if you wanted to search for information relating to the company Nike, you could type in #JustDoIt into the search bar and you'll find all sorts of things about Nike. If you were looking for content related to self-improvement, you could search #selfimprovement and see everything that comes up. In Chapter 3, you will discover how you can use hashtags to drive traffic to your account and boost your sales.

Posting the Perfect Tweet

With everything you've discovered so far, use this checklist to make sure that you have mastered the art of posting the perfect tweet:

1. Post engaging, interactive content—don't be mundane or boring
2. Never complain or act negatively
3. Entertain or educate
4. Keep it short
5. Use at least 1 hashtag
6. Integrate any trending keywords into your post
7. Use only 120-125 characters so you can leave room for retweets

Growing a Follower Base

Now that you are armed with the knowledge to send out effective, engaging, and timely tweets, it is time to learn how to grow your follower base so that you can interact with thousands! I have seen accounts with 50k+ followers. What an audience! In this section, I will teach you how to build your audience and get more people to follow you in the most efficient and quickest ways possible.

There are some general rules that you can follow to help keep a steady flow of followers streaming on to your page. Think of it as the "more in, more out" rule. If you want more users to interact on your page, send out more tweets in the form of a question. If you want more people to mention you, start mentioning them first. Most importantly, if you want more followers... **follow more people**. Following more people is not the golden rule for reaching thousands of followers but it is one of the main strategies!

When you follow a user, that person will be sent an email or an alert letting them know that you just followed them. Of all the users you follow, at least 10% will follow you back. Up to 50% of users who look at your profile will follow you back if they are interested in your material (you will learn the importance of this in a few steps). While only 2% of people who you follow will re-tweet your content, this is still very powerful. There is this principle called "The Rule of 52", which states that for every person you know, they have 52 connections and for every connection, that person has another 52 connections. That is how many things go viral on the internet. When a user retweets your material, they are sending it out to all of *their* friends too. Keep in mind that up to 90% of users you follow might take no action at all—that's okay. You just have to push yourself to keep trying until you get the results you want.

When you go looking for users to follow, the key is to make sure that those followers are **relevant** to you. Remember—up to 50% of those you follow will follow you back if they're interested in you. I am an author, so many of the users I follow are people who like to read. I also write for niches, such as health and fitness, business and finance and peak performance, so I tend to follow users who are somehow related or interested in these fields. This way, when I post content, I know that the majority of my audience will have an interest in what I am saying, promoting, or giving away for free.

Now, are you ready for the ultimate **secret** on how to get 10k, 20k, and more followers? You'll be surprised; it can actually be quite easy when paired with the right tools. **The trick is to find accounts that are very similar to yours.** Make sure each account has a large follower base and that it is a legit profile. Look for things about that profile that are similar to yours. Since I am a self-improvement author, let's say that I look at the Twitter account of Tony Robbins, a well-known life coach. He's not specifically an author but he does have the power to move mountains for other people, so I already know that his audience consists of people who love to learn and improve themselves. Now, I could go on his profile and click on the "followers" tab. Then I could go down the list and click "follow" on every user who follows him. That is called the manual follow. Just don't follow too many people at once, especially if you have a new account. It is generally safe to follow 25-30 people per day with a new account. Once you have established yourself over several months, then you can start increasing this to 100 or more follows per day.

Sounds easy right? It is, but there is one slight problem—big name accounts tend to have *a lot* of followers. Tony Robbins has 2.46 MILLION followers! If I went through his entire list and followed each person individually, I'd be on Twitter until the day I die. Luckily, there is a solution to that small snag!

The solution is to use a program that automates your following process for you. Twitter does not make this process easy and has actually eliminated many of the free programs that previously let you automate following. However, there are still ways to get around this. Most programs that allow you to do this are paid, but most of them are inexpensive and come with a one-time cost, so the best way to see this payment is as an investment in yourself.

One of the best products on the market for this is ManageFlitter. This powerful tool lets you follow up to 1,000 users within minutes. Moreover, it can filter accounts to ensure that you're only following live, legitimate people/businesses. It can help you find useful accounts using keywords, location, interests, and other factors. This program can also give you a better idea of what time to contact your followers. Finally, you can schedule tweets in advance and have them sent out automatically.

There are many tools that you can use to get more followers, but this one is the most powerful out there. In just 5 minutes, this program can get you at least 3,000 followers. So if I wanted to follow all 2.46 million of Tony Robbins' followers, I would be able to do it faster and easier with this program. The program is also fairly inexpensive and it offers different packages, including a free account that you can try. If you are serious about Twitter, then this is a must have addition to your Twitter weapons arsenal!

I want to make it clear that I am not trying to "sell" or "advertise" ManageFlitter or any of the other programs I mention... ManageFlitter and the others are just truly the best out there. Check out this video, How To Use ManageFlitter to Bulk Follow People on Twitter, to see how ridiculously easy this program makes it for you. Honestly, without an automated program, you will be at your computer for many, many long and boring hours trying to manually follow users. I don't know about you but that is enough to drive me crazy! It may be a free method, but it is not ideal. Remember, time is money! You could be using the time that ManageFlitter or a similar program saves you by working on your content, brand, business, products, etc.—the things that really count and bring you the best results or the most money.

If you optimize your page correctly, do enough research to find accounts that are relevant to your industry, and devote your time and efforts into your material, ManageFlitter or a similar paid program will no doubt pay for itself in no time. For the best results, it is important to follow each and every step that you've learned so far, because it all comes together in the end.

Important Note: Twitter has something called "following limits," which puts a restriction on how many people you can follow per account per day. An average account is allowed to follow about 1,000 people a day. A newer account, or one that might come off as spam, has a lower limit, usually only around 100 or 200 per day, but I recommend 25-30 per day for new accounts. Though sometimes they will issue you a warning for your first offense, it is very crucial to pay attention to how many people you are following per day. If you break this rule too many times, Twitter will suspend your account and all of your time, money, and efforts will be rendered useless.

Chapter 2: How To Successfully Manage Your Twitter Account

So you're starting to gets hundreds of followers—now what? One thing you may notice is that your Twitter news feed may begin to get overwhelming. Before you started to work on growing your follower base, you may have added random people: friends, family, colleagues, or anyone who was willing to follow you. You may have also followed your favorite celebrities or musicians. These might be people who you no longer need on your news feed, especially if you're trying to narrow your follower base to a specific niche.

Then of course you have those who send out 5 tweets an hour instead of 5 tweets a day—on any type of social media platform, those types of users can get annoying. If you find it hard to read and manage your news feed, using Twitter can easily become frustrating and you may feel tempted to quit—DON'T! Twitter is such an underestimated, powerful social media tool and it is too valuable to throw away. There are things that you can do to better manage your news feed and account so that you can get the most out of this platform without having to sift through spam, annoying tweeters and anything else unnecessary.

This is where some more great third-party programs come in. One is TweetDeck. This programs allows you to easily organize your page, ranging from column-based lists, trends, mentions and searches. If you have multiple accounts, you can use this program to organize each one in a separate column. You can download this program to your computer or mobile device and is definitely recommended. TweetDeck also allows you to automatically schedule your tweets ahead of time free of charge.

Hootsuite is another popular tool that you can use to manage your page. Unlike TweetDeck, Hootsuite is a web-based application and ranges from free to paid memberships. It has similar features but allows you to integrate other social media sites such as LinkedIn and Facebook.

ManageFlitter has an excellent "unfollow" tool. This feature shows you users that you are following who don't follow you back, post, have a profile picture, etc. Watch ManageFlitter's Unfollow Walkthrough video to see just how easy it is to rid your Twitter account of useless, negative, or spammy accounts.

If you're using Twitter on your smart-phone, there is a handy little app called TweetCaster that can manage your news feed by hiding tweets as opposed to unfollowing that user. Twitterific is an app for Apple products that you can use to filter trending topics, hashtags, and usernames as well as send push notifications to your device whenever you are mentioned.

SocialOomph is another popular Twitter-management tool that focuses on boosting productivity and automation. Using this tool, which has both a free and paid version, you can schedule tweets in advance, track keywords, reuse drafts, keep your direct message inbox clean and link up to 5 different accounts. You can even erase all of your tweets and start from scratch! The paid version allows you to automatically follow back a user who has followed you. It also allows you to directly send a message to new follows (which can be great for marketing), find new users through a keyword search, sort users into lists, all while offering full quality and spam control.

More Account Management Tips:

1. Log into each account at least once a day
2. Check your mentions and direct messages
3. Filter spam
4. Respond to important messages ASAP

5. Use at least 1 automation program to regulate each account
6. Plan content one month ahead of time

Chapter 3: Marketing And Making Money On Twitter

After reading Chapter 1 and 2, I am sure you can already understand the power of Twitter. It goes beyond any other social media site so that you can reach out to nearly anybody in the world—even celebrities! That being said, Twitter is a powerful tool for marketing your business or product. It is truly incredible what just one tweet can do if it goes viral! Truly amazing!

The Main Method to Boost Sales and Traffic

There is one marketing method on Twitter that is still slightly untapped. It does take some time and effort but the return can be amazing. The key is to become the solution to other peoples' problems. What do I mean by that?

Let's pretend that I am getting ready to market my latest self-improvement book but I am not sure how to go about it. What I could do is research the questions that people are asking online about the topic of the book. My latest book happens to be on leadership, so I will use that for this example. I could search for questions on any online forum, such as Yahoo Answers, but since this book is about Twitter I will focus on using Twitter. What I would do is find out who needs help with leadership. Then I would tweet them a solution—something about my book. If they are having leadership trouble, my book stands as a potential solution.

In the Twitter search bar, I would type in a short phrase about leadership and add a question mark at the end (signifying that I am looking for users who are asking real questions). For this example, I typed in "I want to be a leader?" After a quick search of the results, I found one young woman who expressed a concern about wanting to become a leader of the alumni for her school. Now I have the option of reaching out to that young woman to make a connection and offer her a solution to her problem. Then I can go back and look for more opportunities. When doing this, try to experiment with the phrases you type into the search bar to get the best results.

Hint: If you use the word "retweet" or phrase "RT" in your response, the odds of it being retweeted stand at 12x's more than if it didn't. If you write "RETWEET" in all caps, it is 23x's more likely to be shared.

Another method you can use is a type of networking—to try and get in with the "big time leaders" in your industry. This method is a little trickier and is not guaranteed, but it would be your loss if you didn't try it. What you can do is create a list of well-known professionals who have a big influence in your field. Research those people and try to connect with them on Twitter. If you can connect with them, try to build your relationship. One good way to do this is either research their personal website or Twitter account and mention something that they're currently involved in. Say something like, "Hey, I just wanted to say congratulations on your newest blog!" or "That's really cool that you're into x—I'm studying that myself," or something along those lines to build rapport. If they don't respond, try following through but don't be too annoying—give it two or three shots and if you don't hear back, move on and try to connect with someone else. As I said, this method can be a little harder to break into, but if you can do it, you can probably make some major connections within your field.

Now, there are some other things you can do to make that method much more powerful, and you are about to discover how!

Using Multiple Accounts to Boost Sales

If your business or service allows it, you can use multiple accounts to boost your sales. Managing multiple accounts may seem difficult, but if you pair them up with one of the great tools mentioned in Chapter 2, you should have no problem keeping track of everything on a single platform. Using multiple accounts to boost sales is a powerful marketing method because it helps you reach more potential customers and it lets you branch off your business into multiple areas. For example, Starbucks has a main Twitter page for "Starbucks", but they also have separate accounts for their Pumpkin Spice Latte beverage, their career opportunities, and their public relations. This method is totally legal and is used by many companies.

Hint: Make sure that each sub-account comes off as legitimate and not spammy. Also, always be sure which account you are logged into before sending out a tweet. It can be pretty embarrassing if you send out a tweet onto the wrong account!

Driving Traffic and Sales With Hashtags

Do you remember how powerful the use of hashtags can be on Twitter? Not only can you use hashtags in a way to capture anyone who searches for a keyword, but you can also use them to market and promote your product or service. Many businesses hold contests in which they give something away in exchange for a tweet that contains a certain hashtag. When done correctly, this can help your product or service reach a huge audience. Just don't use too many hashtags in one tweet or your audience may become too broad.

To make the most out of hashtags for your own product or service, use this action plan:

1. Create a spreadsheet and save it as a list of hashtags that are related to your business.
2. Search Twitter for existing hashtags. See if you can find all the relevant ones and copy them into your spreadsheet.
3. Use these categories to find hashtags: trending topics, content, events, location, lifestyle and product.

Example: I am an author, so I would be looking to gather hashtags that are related to authoring and writing as well as the content of my books. One of the most trending hashtags that is related to writing is #amwriting. So if I was to send out a tweet about how I am working on my latest book and how I want my audience to be excited about it, I could post something like this:

Looking to improve your #leadership skills? Stay tuned for my new #ebook coming soon! #amwriting

With a tweet like that, I could reach anybody who searches for "amwriting," which is likely a lot of people since it's trending and I could get my audience excited for the book before it even comes out.

I can also tweet about my book when it goes free on Kindle, so I could use event-related hashtags such as #kindle and #free to let my audience know that there is an event happening where they can get my latest book for free.

Lastly, I will give an example of a content-related hashtag tweet. Let's say that I am going to tweet about my leadership book. I could send out a tweet that looks like this:

Did you know that a great #leader often takes short walks to #destress? Find out why and more in my latest #ebook on #Leadership [insert media].

Take a few minutes and see if you can come up with a tweet for each hashtag category that is relevant to your product or service.

Using Different Style Tweets to Appeal to Your Audience

Finally, you can use different approaches in the style of your tweets to appeal to a wide audience. There are about 3 common types of tweets that you can tailor to a specific audience or use to attract new members of your audience. Each tweet is meant to stir up different emotions in different people.

The first type of tweet is the niche tweet. This type calls out a specific niche. For example, you could target "men and fitness" or "women and heart health." For example, if you target parents, you can reach out to men and women at the same time because both men and women are parents. Here is an example of a good niche tweet:

You won't believe this #1 trick to get your #kids to go to bed early [insert link to article or other media]

If you were to post that tweet, you would likely get clicks from parents of both genders who have an interest in getting their children to sleep early. If you really wanted to reach this market, you could do a Twitter search to find parents who are specifically having this problem.

The second type of tweet is the entertaining tweet. This type of tweet is meant to be fun and positive. Everybody wants to experience feelings of positivity and fun, so you can really reach a lot of people with this method. Interestingly, entertaining tweets tend to get 3x's the amount of retweets. There is some room here for you to use your imagination for this type of tweet. I've found that posting inspirational quotes can get you a lot of retweets and thus reach a wider audience. Don't use any links to media for these tweets—just focus on pure content. Other ideas could be to use jokes, share a fun memory from your day, or to just share an insight. The ideas for this are endless.

The third type of tweet is the controversial tweet. This type of tweet is meant to stir up minor debates among your followers (avoid politics or any other touchy issues that can really get people going—the point is just to stir up a small amount of emotion). However, a little bit of controversy can evoke emotions and responses from a large mass of people.

Remember the perfect tweet formula:

1/5 educational/how-to
1/5 inspirational
1/5 fun
1/5 retweeted
1/5 self-promotional

One Last Note: Don't Sell Directly!

The last thing that your audience on Twitter wants is a sales pitch. Don't try to shove your product or service down anyone's throat. Instead, focus on building relationships and being a good friend. When you do that, your sales will likely come naturally. Become the "go-to" person in your industry. Provide "how-to's" and instructional material—more often than not, people will try something themselves, fail, and then turn to you, the professional, for help. Become the person or business that your audience trusts. Get inside of your audience's head and figure out what they want and how you can provide it.

Twitter Affiliate Marketing

Now that you know how to market your product or service on Twitter, you can go ahead and put those principles into place to boost your sales and make money on

Twitter. One of the best ways to make money on Twitter without selling your own products or services is to get into Twitter affiliate marketing.

Affiliate marketing is a process by which you can earn a commission by promoting and directly selling the products or services of someone else. This process benefits both the company and the consumer, because each party gets something out of an affiliate sale.

First and foremost, it is important to apply a marketing strategy to your affiliate marketing campaigns. You can't just pick a company to be an affiliate for—you have to find a target audience, be engaging, and sell indirectly, just as if you were selling your own product or service. Keep your affiliate products relevant to the purpose of your page so you do not come off as a spammer.

Reputable Affiliate Sites You Can Use With Twitter

SponsoredTweets is not actually an affiliate site but you can use it to make money on Twitter. What you do is you link up with advertisers who may be interested in having you tweet advertisements for pay. It is almost like a freelance business, as you get to set your price for every tweet sent out. You can also pick the category in which you want to tweet in. If any advertisers are interested, they will contact you to get started.

Clickbank is a good resource to find many kinds of products that you can promote as an affiliate. The vendors that you meet through this page will provide you with all of the marketing materials you need to help sell the products, such as sales letters, links, or email marketing content. All products from Clickbank come with a 60-day guarantee, which makes it more appealing for consumers.

Linkshare is another good resource for those who want to market affiliated products to a niche audience. One of Linkshare's best feature is that it helps affiliates and vendors work together to optimize sales on both ends. Linkshare is one of the most top-rated affiliated resources out there.

Paidpertweet is sort of like SponsoredTweets in which you set a price to tweet for other companies and create a buzz. Advertisers on this website will hire you to tweet anything from press releases to actual products and services.

The Amazon Affiliate Program can be a powerful way to make money on Twitter, especially if your profile is designed for a niche audience. With this program, you provide the links to products to other users. If another user clicks on that link and purchases a product through it, you will earn a commission of up to 15%. If you're an expert in your field with a large, trusting audience, this program has the potential to be very lucrative for you. To be able to tweet amazon affiliate links, your profile needs to be verified, which will be indicated by a check mark in the picture of your profile. There is nothing you can do to become verified besides use twitter regularly and hope that twitter will verify you. This can take a very long time. However, if your twitter account is unverified by Twitter, you can put the affiliate product on your blog or website, then have the twitter link go to that product on your blog or website, and when the customer clicks on your website or blog, that is when your amazon affiliate link will kick in.

If you have an audience who might appeal to events, then Tiqiq might be a good affiliate program to check out. Here, you can sell tickets to all sorts of events across the country and earn up to 12% commission on each sale. Throw in some hashtags on these tweets and you might find yourself with a lot more traffic on your page.

You can do some of your own research to find the best affiliate marketing program for your account. Just treat each tweet as if you were marketing your own product or service and you are bound to be successful. Read on to Chapter 4 to discover how to put everything together for ultimate Twitter success!

Chapter 4: Putting It All Together In An Action Plan For Success

Now it's time to learn the most exciting part—putting it all together. Now you know how to master nearly every part of Twitter as well as how to use some great third-party programs to harness the best results. Now it is just a matter of creating a step-by-step plan to put it into action. Let's get started, there's no time to lose!

Step 1: Create Your Twitter "Business Plan"

Before you do anything, you must have a general, underlying business plan for your Twitter account that can serve as your business plan. This is so you can make sure you have all the basics ready before you begin marketing. Ask yourself these questions:

1. Do I have a Twitter account? If no, make one. If yes, go to next question.
2. Does my Twitter account need to be fixed up?
3. How engaged am I with my current follower base?

Write down the answer to those questions and be completely honest with yourself. Nobody but you will know the answers. Now, I want you to take 10 minutes and write down **3 to 5 goals** that you want to achieve on Twitter. These goals will serve as your main motivators. You can always refer back to these goals when you're working on optimizing your account.

At this time, I want you to go into your account and make sure that your bio is filled out, that you have an appropriate picture up, and that you've utilized your header space in the best way possible for your brand. Do you have a call to action? Put it in the header!

Review your handle and make sure that it is catchy and memorable. Don't forget to fill out your location—do some research first to see what users are looking for (remember, NYC vs New York City?).

If you have a website, make sure you add that to the website box.

Take a few minutes and evaluate your color scheme. Is it simple and pleasing to the eye?

Step 2: Planning Your Interaction Strategy

Now that you have your goals and basic profile areas filled out, it is time to figure out your interaction strategy. Remember, Twitter is all about real time interaction, so it is important to master this area. You don't necessarily have to be in front of your computer to interact with other followers, thanks to the great automation programs you've learned about, but without a strategy in place, it won't work.

First, answer this important question: **What is my communication style?** Are you going to be the account who just performs one-way communication or will you have a two-way communication style? (Hint: Two-way communication is usually best for stirring up interaction).

What is the style and tone of your tweets? Will you use cliffhanger tweets? Funny tweets? Controversial? Helpful?

What type of media will you share most? Can you find any ways to integrate your other media accounts to Twitter? For example, you can make it so that any videos you upload to YouTube automatically get sent to Twitter. Tweets with pictures in them are also much more likely to be checked out.

What is your response strategy? How will you respond to comments, direct messages, and mentions? How will you handle negativity and complaints?

Step 3: Scheduling and Timing

Next, I want you to do this exercise: go through your materials that are related to your brand/business and use a word processor to write out 5 tweets. Write up one "how-to/educational" tweet, find one inspirational quote or picture, find a fun or light article, joke, etc, write a self-promotional tweet, and then find another user to retweet. Do these sound familiar? They should, because they came straight from the "1/5 formula" that you previously read about!

Now pick an automation program and I will walk you through scheduling and timing. You may already have an automation software downloaded and installed but for easier purposes, let's use Buffer since it is free and easy to use. If you haven't done so already, sign up and link your Twitter account. You can link your other accounts later.

Add each tweet that you previously wrote up to your que. With the free version, you can upload and schedule 4 in advance, so just pick the four that you want to use. Then, go to "schedule" at the top of the page and you will come to page where you can set 4 different times for each tweet to go out. Do you remember the most important times to send out tweets?

Set one to go out between 7pm and 8pm. Set another one to go out between 1pm and 2pm. Set the third one to go out between 5pm and 6pm. Finally, set the last one to go out sometime between 9pm and 10pm. Once you have more time to experiment and get to know some of the other programs, you can really do some hardcore research and narrow your times based on location and other factors. If you plan on doing more tweets, then try starting out using TweetDeck.

Step 4: Create Your Hashtag Plan

Don't forget about hashtags—they can really make or break your tweets and their retweet potential. For this step, you can jump right into this exercise:

Create a list of hashtags that you think you can use based off your brand. Open up a spreadsheet in your word processor and start making lists. Make 6 different columns and label each one "trending," "event," "lifestyle," "content," "location," and "product." Put each hashtag you can think of in its respectful category. This strategy may take some time, especially if you're first starting out.

One good idea to collect hashtags is to just keep your eyes out on Twitter. Every time you see a hashtag that you can add to your list, write it down and add it when you can. If you can break down your hashtag categories even more, do it! For example, I am an author, so I have a collection of hashtags that are directly related to being an author. If I want to tweet about one of my books, I will use hashtags that relate to the genre of the book.

Step 5: Start Building Your Follower Base

Go back to Chapter 1 and check out some of the resources that I recommended for building your follower base and automating follows. You are welcome to try and manually build your follower base, which doesn't take up too much time in the beginning! In the meantime, make a list of the top 10 key influencers of your field. Reach out to them and look at their follower list to get an idea of how to build your niche audience. You can also follow their followers, which is a strategy most twitter pros use. Once you've got all that information, pick a program and see how many followers you can get each week.

Step 6: Figure Out Your Account Management Strategy

Once your follower base starts growing, you are going to want to know how to manage your news feed. Go ahead and experiment with some of the great account management tools that you've already read about. A good one to start with is Hootsuite because there is a free version and a lot of support, so you can play around with it and then upgrade to the paid version once your follower base really starts hitting the high thousands. You can also hire a virtual assistant from sites like Odesk and Elance to manage your twitter account if you find yourself getting overwhelmed.

Follow those steps and you will no doubt be on your way to becoming a master of Twitter. Some steps can be done within seconds and others will take some time, so don't expect to get amazing results overnight. Give yourself at least a few months. See how you're doing. If you're getting the results you want, narrow in and see what's working best for you. If you're not happy with your results, reevaluate your strategy and see if you can change anything around. Remember, getting a powerful twitter account is based on more of a grinding technique. That is, you need to pick a strategy and use it every day. You won't get super quick results at first, but overtime, the results will be amazing!

Chapter 5: The Best Twitter Resources

Best Twitter Programs and Apps

Tweetium is an exclusive app for Windows 8 that allows users to amazingly customize their account and news feed as well as make it easy to use Twitter with its snap-mode option. This app costs $3 and is also available for Windows phones, making it a great option for those who are often mobile.

Tweeki is a great free program that helps users better manage their account. The interface is smooth and it has the basic management features—grouping, listing, and organizing direct messages. Other features of this program include multiple-account management, quick access to the tweet composer, and push notifications.

Tweetro+ is a great program for Windows that can be beneficial to those who manage multiple Twitter accounts.

Sobees is another free management program that lets you manage all of social media accounts at once. It has some basic functions such as a retweeing ability and list management tools. Though it is not as powerful as some Twitter management software, it is definitely a nice little gem.

TweetDeck is a powerful management app for Mac and Windows. Its entire interface allows users to customize their time lines with easy list management and advanced hashtag/event/topic tracking. This powerhouse program allows users to schedule tweets in advance, stream their news feed in real-time format, and mute/delete unwanted followers. This is one of my favorite programs.

Janetter is the best program for those who are big on visual aesthetics. This program allows users to fully customize themes from scratch or pick from a pre-made collection. The program also comes with basic account management features such as link shortening, multiple-account management and muting options.

Twtrland is the perfect tool for connecting with users who are relevant to your business or purpose. This powerful tool organizes all profiles into 60,000 categories that you can further refine to build the perfect target audience and connect with the most influential people in your field.

Commun.it is one of Twitter's best relationship management tools. This tool categorizes your account into 3 sections: your top influencers, your top supporters and your most engaged followers. This program will help you manage your most important relationships by sending out alerts and reminders to interact with these people. There is so much more to Commun.it and it can really help you regulate your relationships on Twitter.

Twitonomy is a powerful tool that you can use to analyze your own account as well as the accounts of others (your competitors, perhaps?). Twitonomy shows you who the account is interacting with the most as well as what times they send out tweets, what tools they use, and which tweets they retweet or favorite. You definitely don't want to miss out on this tool.

Hootsuite is one of the hottest tools for Twitter. It combines the power of tweet scheduling, information filtering, and details on those who are following you. There is a free and paid version and although you will get better results with the paid version, the free version still offers amazing functionality.

Tweepi is an awesome account management tool that utilizes statistics to help you better control your news feed and follower base. This program also comes with a blog that contains helpful tips and tricks that help you to become a master at managing your Twitter account.

Buffer is a basic program that allows you to schedule tweets in advance. You can use it on a web browser or take it to go on your smart phone. Not only can you schedule tweets in advance with this program, but it will also suggests tweets for you—which can be very helpful. You can also use this program to send out information on any other social media platforms that you have.

Topsy is a tweet search engine that you can use to go through every tweet from 2006 until the present. This useful tool can be a great source of research and is better than a general search engine because it specifically revolves around Twitter.

Mention.net is a helpful tool for monitoring your keywords. Not everyone mentions you by username when sharing your content, so that is where this tool fills in the gap. Mention.net even allows you to monitor the blog posts of your competitors so you can stay on top of your game.

Cybranding is your key to hashtag analytics. With this program, you can enter any hashtag and then let the software analyze the statistics for you.

Social Oomph is an awesome program that features a tweet que. You can compile a collection of tweets and the program Soocial Oomph will help you pick out one to send. This program also has almost every management feature you can think of—from keyword tracking to auto-following. There is a free and paid version but it is definitely worth checking out, as it is a very powerful "all in one" tool.

SocialBro is the perfect tool for timing your tweets in a strategic manner. This tool will analyze your followers to find out what times they are mostly online. Then you can use that information to plan when you send out your tweets. With the right amount of logical thinking, this tool can really help you perfectly time your tweets.

NeedTagger is a great tool that you can use to track and find business leads. You can also track leads through customer service issues and product mentions. This tool can go very well when you're trying to boost sales by becoming the solution to peoples' problems

Videos

Best Time to Tweet on Twitter – Twitter For Business 2014

50 Twitter Power Tips

Twitter Marketing Tips: How To Use Twitter Lists

Twitter Marketing Tips: Twitter Advanced Search

What is a Hashtag and How Do I Use Them on Twitter?

Tweet Content Ideas

Alltop.com – Trending news topics

PopUrls.com – More trending news topics

Google Trends – Current trending topics plus trends by month and location

Trending Now – Yahoo's source of trending topics

Visual Aesthetic and Graphics Optimized For Twitter

Twitpic

Twitcoverz

Twitheaders

MorgueFile – 100% completely free stock photos for commercial use

Conclusion

Thank you again for downloading this book!

I hope this book was able to help you to discover what it takes to create an amazing, successful Twitter account to market your products or services with. Now that you know just how powerful Twitter is as both a social media platform as well as a marketing tool, I hope that you put in the time necessary to become truly successful! The exponential power of twitter can be truly staggering, so be sure to use all the tips and strategies in this book to maximize your own success potential! Remember, people are sending out 140 million tweets every day, so it is important to come up with a killer marketing strategy that will set you apart from the rest and push you to the top!

The next step is to start working on Twitter as soon as you can! The sooner you get started, the more people you can reach and the sooner you will become a master. Refer back to the step-by-step plan and personalize it to your business or brand. Go back and experiment with some of the great third-party programs listed throughout this book and in Chapter 5. Without utilizing at least some of these programs, it will likely be much harder for you to climb to the top. Do some of your own research, give some programs a try and figure out which ones will work best for you and your business.

Remember, you cannot become a master of Twitter overnight. It will take time and it will take a lot of dedication and passion (even though most of the process will be automated). However, you simply cannot miss out on all the opportunities that Twitter provides to you. If you ever find yourself discouraged or bored, I recommend keeping some sort of reminder of your passion or goals nearby your work area. It could be an inspirational quote, a picture, or the house of your dreams... any time you are feeling discouraged or overwhelmed, take a glance at it and remind yourself why you are becoming a Twitter master in the first place.

I hope this book was able to help you and I wish you the best of luck in building up your Twitter account. Feel free to follow me on Twitter at @AcesEbooks to see all my newest promotions and free e-book downloads.

Finally, if you discovered at least one thing that has helped you or that you think would be beneficial to someone else, be sure to take a few seconds to easily post a quick positive review on Amazon. As an author, your positive feedback is desperately needed so that I can continue to provide you with **The BEST E-Books At The best Price!** Your highly valuable five star reviews are like a river of golden joy flowing through a sunny forest of mighty trees and beautiful flowers! *To do your good deed in making the world a better place by helping others with your valuable insight, just* **CLICK HERE**

Preview Of "Money: The Top 100 Best Ways To Make And Manage Money"

I want to thank you and congratulate you for downloading the book: Money- The Top 100 Best Ways To Make And Manage Money.

This book will provide you with time tested and proven methods to bring more money into your life. There are things that you can do on a daily basis that will pay huge dividends for your financial wellbeing over the long term. In this book you will also discover some of the biggest mistakes that people make with money and how to avoid them yourself. You will also find out the keys to money management success that the wealthiest people in the world use on a regular basis. If you're not happy with your yearly income and are finally ready to do something about it, then this is the book for you!

Money might be printed on a fancy piece of paper, but its importance in everyday life cannot be denied! However, what you may not know is that money doesn't have to control you—you can learn how to control it. Have you ever lost sleep over not knowing whether your bills were going to get paid? I know I have and it's a horrible feeling. When you master good money-handling habits, eventually all of your financial worries can simply melt away. You don't have to be a Wall Street genius to utilize the strategies in this book. There are many great ways to better manage your money and there are even more ways to generate additional income! The key is to discover which strategies work best for you, and then to implement them intelligently.

Why is it so important to master money? Well, it's true that you can fall into a pretty bad pitfall if you don't—you could lose the roof over your head, the car that gets you to and from work, the electricity that keeps your devices running, and the gas that keeps you warm at night. Although it is important to not let money control your life and you should always be grateful for the things in your life that money *can't* buy, the reality is that money makes the world go round. Money is required to raise children, buy food, purchase clothes, acquire the latest gadgets and so much more that keeps your life going smoothly.

If money is in short supply, it can often lead to mental stress, relationship problems, and a variety of other negative consequences. Mental stress from lack of money can tire you out, wear you down, and make you physically sick. It can take away from your best performances and it can determine whether you keep a job, a relationship and a happy life. Some people let their money problems go unresolved for so long that it ends up entirely consuming everything they have. Unresolved money problems can come back to haunt you in the future, too. They can ruin your credit score and make it harder for you to take out loans and mortgages. Once your credit has gone bad, then it is even more expensive for you to get around in daily life!

By learning how to master the art of handling money, your life can be so much better! You'll never have to worry about late bill payments, emergency medical bills, car maintenance, or anything else that currently seems to suck the hard-earned money right out of your pocket. You'll be able to focus on more important aspects of your life, such as spending time with your family, traveling and exploring new places, enjoying your favorite hobby and anything else you've ever dreamed of! You'll be able to afford the extras and not worry one bit! So get ready to take control of your finances once and for all! Your journey to financial freedom begins here.

Chapter 1: Wiring Your Brain For Financial Success

Before you can even think about earning and saving more money, you have to mentally prepare yourself first. Has anyone ever told you, "it's all in your head?" When it comes to money, that's nearly the truth! Before we dive into the different ways you can save and earn more money, it is crucial that you learn how to handle money in your brain first. Once you have mastered this, you will find it much easier to handle money in real life.

How to Grow Your Income

When it comes to you and your money, it is important to remember that your income can only go as far as you can. Do you know anybody who has ever won the lottery? Studies actually have found that people who have suddenly won or inherited large amounts of money often end up losing it all after several years—and it's likely not a coincidence. In many of these cases, these people did not have what it takes to handle their money, mentally. Interestingly, people who have worked themselves into being millionaires can often incur financial tragedies and still manage to get back on their feet within a short period of time.

Think about it—if you believe that you don't deserve a lot of money, will you be successful in handling it? If you have a shopping addiction and you do nothing to overcome it, what will your wallet look like? Does your character reflect your income? The point is that your financial situation will often reflect who you are as a person—the more successful you are in personal growth, the more your earning potential can be. If you're the type of person who has the ability to exert willpower and discipline when it comes to kicking bad habits, going after goals, and being honest with yourself about your finances, chances are you'll be much more well-off financially.

They key to setting yourself up for financial success is to start from within. It is very easy to dream of becoming a millionaire, living in a mansion, and driving behind the wheel of a brand new car—but first, you must prepare yourself to get all of those things. Money doesn't grow on trees but it does grow from desire and ambition. Think back to school when you learned about cause and effect—there is an effect for every cause—your weight is an effect of what you eat, your knowledge is an effect of your desire to learn, and your money is an effect of what you do to earn and manage it.

I have a story to share that can help you gain a better perspective on this. My friend once worked in the quick service restaurant industry as a manager. One thing that she noticed among most of her workers was that they were not happy about their pay. They would often complain about not getting raises or not getting enough hours but she began to notice a pattern. The same people who complained never sought to do anything about their complaints. They would just do the bare minimum requirements of their job and then go home. They never looked to go above and beyond to prove to their upper management that they were worthy of what they felt they deserved. Even when they had dreams of being successful in other areas of employment, they would never take the effort or initiative to go after those dreams, even when encouraged to do so.

What set my friend aside from her co-workers was that she had the determination and persistence that it took to move up the financial ladder—to get into management, she didn't even wait for the offer—she went out and became certified on her own to give herself an edge. Then, eventually, she wasn't happy about her income at the restaurant either and decided that she deserved more than what she was getting. So, she went out, bought some business books, and launched her own business, finally able to break the roof that was blocking her earning potential and she was finally able to leave the restaurant industry. It didn't even take a degree in business for her to do that.

The moral of the story is that you are the only person who can change the way your money comes to you and stays with you. The great news is that *anyone* can learn how to wire their brains for ultimate financial success. All it takes is a couple of small, simple changes that you can easily implement into your life by making them habits.

Review Your Emotions. Your emotions can be one of the most influential factors that determine where you go in life. As many experts have theorized, your thoughts lead to feelings, your feelings lead to actions, and your actions lead to results. The key is to understand what is driving your feelings, as your feelings are what start the chain of results. The way your emotions are toward money can be very influencing over how you end up handling it. Think about how money was viewed in your household while you were growing up—did you ever hear your parents or guardians say things such as, "money is the root of all evil" or "rich people are stingy, greedy people who aren't like us?" If you grew up hearing those things in person or on TV, than there is a good chance that you are letting your emotions take charge of your finances as an adult. Luckily, there are ways to change your emotions toward money.

Special Exercise—Take out a notebook and write down your thoughts on how you and your family viewed money while you were growing up. Just try to get out any negative things that you heard about it. This will help you raise your awareness about your emotions toward money. Once you've done that, write down your thoughts on how those beliefs may have influenced the way you view money now. One helpful thing you can do is say something out loud to counter those beliefs. For example, if you grew up hearing that "Money is the root of all evil," tell yourself, "Having more money allows me to do more good in the world." You can also do quick positive affirmations whenever your mind may be going negative or anytime you want to start building a solid wealth foundation in your mind. Some examples of positive wealth building affirmations are: "Money comes to me quickly and easily." Or "I am a money magnet." Go ahead and make up your own affirmation and repeat it to yourself regularly. One of my favorite times to do this is on my daily walk.

Review Your Financial Habits. Your habits are the second biggest factor in influencing how you manage your money. <u>Habits</u> are things that you do automatically, so if you have bad financial habits, chances are your money management is poor. For example, if you just always have to buy something when you go to the store, you'll have to break that habit to avoid spending more money than you should, especially if you could be getting a better deal online or somewhere else. If you're used to living off other people, that is definitely a habit that you should break because one day, you might wind up on your own, and you will probably have no idea how to handle money wisely. On the other hand, if you can resist buying something every time you go to a store or if you are working toward becoming financially independent by furthering your knowledge, searching for higher-paying jobs, etc, then you will have some great habits and your money-handling skills will tend to be greater.

Special Exercise—Think and write about your bad habits concerning money. Do you tend to ignore your bank statements? Are you often late on your bill payments? Do you carry cash, cards, or both and how does that impact your spending? Do you have a savings account? Do you spend a lot of money on things that you know are unhealthy? Try to think of the bad habits that will affect you the most negatively in the future. Next, carefully consider each one and ask yourself out loud how that habit has adversely affected your wallet. From each bad habit, analyze the consequences and learn from your mistake. Tell yourself out loud, "I can and I will change my bad money-handling habits." Be 100% honest with yourself, as nobody will know about these thoughts except for you.

Review Your Specific Beliefs About Money. Finally, you must dig deep and grasp the roots of what is causing your most specific, emotional belief about money. When you were little, what do remember experiencing that concerned money? Many people grow up believing false assumptions, such as "men are the breadwinners," or "women are meant to stay home and take care of the house," or "money is what makes people get divorced," etc. Whatever assumptions and specific emotional memories you have of money can seriously influence the way you handle it.

Special Exercise: Think about the most significant emotional memory you have had concerning money and write about how it may have impacted your life today. Then, say something out loud to try and distance yourself from that memory. Saying something along the lines of, "I will not let this memory affect how I handle money today."

Wire Your Brain Continuously. Once you have consciously made the decision to distance yourself from your previous beliefs about money, the next step is to wire your brain to start handling money better. Think about what you're making now and how you're spending it. Can you do better? Are you struggling to pay your bills? Answering all of these questions is very important for properly reprogramming your brain to handle money. Once you have answered those questions it's time to start using positive affirmations to combat your old negative thinking behavior. You also want to program your brain for financial abundance. So you can visualize money coming to you in all sorts of different ways and you could also try to think of one hundred dollar bills as one dollar bills to help program your brain for financial abundance. I would also highly recommend Hypnosis for those who are serious about programming their brain for financial success. My favorite source for great audios is hypnosis downloads. I personally use and can highly recommend "The Millionaire Mindset" bundle package or you can try: "Overcome Fear of Money."

If you really want to go to the next level of brain mind technology and program positive associations of money into your brain, than I would also recommend subliminal messaging. There is a great program that I use on my computer every day called Subliminal Power. This program is super easy to use and it allows you to custom make your own subliminal messages. Another great feature is that you can add pictures to the subliminal messages and the program comes with some great brainwave music as well.

How to Set Financial Goals

Once you have mentally prepared yourself for financial success, the next step is to set your goals and get to work on them. When setting financial goals, it is important to set short-term, mid-term, and long-term goals. For example, a short-term financial goal could be to pay off the last remaining balance of your car loan. An example of a mid-term goal could be to have three thousand dollars in a bank account for use in emergencies. An example of a long-term goal could be to have all your debt paid off in three years.

A great way to stick to your goals is to have a visual chart. Here is a worksheet that you can easily copy down on a piece of paper to help yourself get started and organized:

	Target Completion Date	**~Total Cost**	**Amount Saved**	**Amount Needed to Finish**
Short-Term Goal				
Mid-Term Goal				
Long-Term Goal				

Next, think about any time in the past where you have set financial goals. Did you achieve them or did you utterly fail? If you failed, think about why that happened and learn from your mistake so that you won't make it again today.

After that, ask yourself the famous question, "**what motivates you?**" If you're not motivated by anything to start changing your financial habits, then you probably will not succeed. Really sit down and think about this question for a while. Many people are motivated to improve their money management skills so they can take more vacations, attract a new love interest, buy a new house or car, buy a boat, send their children to private school or college, or have enough money to take care of a parent later in life. Those are just a few common examples, your motivation may be entirely different, and that's okay! Just make absolutely sure to not skip this step until you have a clear idea in your mind as to why you are going to do the things you do in order to be financially free.

Finally, review your goal chart and make sure that your goals are challenging yet realistic. Don't set goals that are too easy and don't set goals that are impossible to reach. Make sure they are logical, easy to track, realistic, and important to you. A great strategy to start off each goal with the phrase: "I will easily..."

If you really want to do your goals like a professional, then I would highly recommend the Goals On Track program. It is by far the best goal setting program that I have ever come across! It e-mails your goals to you daily for easy reference, it allows you to attach pictures to your goals, easily tracks goal progress and the program also comes with a vision board and journal.

Once you have made your goals, it is time to start going out there and getting them accomplished! But wait—there's more to rewiring your brain when it comes to money management...

Prepare a Budget

Preparing your own personalized budget is important so that you can become aware of just how much money you're spending each month and how much money you will need to save. Many people turn to professional financial advisers but you can easily make your own perfect budget right here in this chapter. All it takes is a few easy steps:

1) **Save Copies of Every Bill You Pay and Take Them Out.** Gather up everything that costs you money each month—rental payment receipts, utility bills, loan payments receipts, and your bank statements. Don't forget to count all expenses like grocery shopping, gas for your car, entertainment, etc. To ensure that you can best keep track of your money, a good idea is to rarely carry cash with you and to pay everything with a debit or credit card—that way, all of your purchases can be tracked onto your bank statement. That idea is totally up to you, as many people have different preferences about methods of payment.

2) **Figure Out Where Your Income is Coming From.** Next, take out your pay stubs or make an approximate calculation of how much money you actually bring home each month. Count anything from rental income,

self-employment money, or anything else that brings money *into* your pocket. Try to be as accurate as possible.

3) **Divide Expenses Into Two Categories.** Next, organize your bills and expenses and allocate them into one of two categories—fixed or variable. You would put expenses that stay the same, such as your rent or your cable bill in the "fixed" category while you would put expenses that can differ from month-to-month, such as dining out expenses, into the "variable" category. This will be helpful in allowing you to make any necessary changes to your budget later on.

4) **Add It All Together.** Now, add up your monthly expenses and compare it to your total monthly income. If your income is more than your expenses, then you're in pretty good shape and you have the freedom to decide whether you need to make any changes to save more. If your expenses are more than your income then you should definitely look and see where you can make some cuts.

5) **Review.** Finally, it is important to review your budget each month as it can be very easy for your bills to fluctuate. For example, your gas bill may be higher in the winter because you will need to use more heat but your electric bill may go down in the summer if you like to spend a lot of time outdoors. By giving yourself a heads up on what your bills are going to look like for the month, you can make smarter spending decisions.

Make Your Own Definition of Money and Its Purpose. The last step in rewiring your brain to look at money differently is to make up your own definition of money. You know what money is, obviously, but what is it to you? How does money serve you? The answer to this question will be different for everyone but when you're answering it, be completely honest with yourself. Nobody but you will know the answer and you don't have to share it with anybody. Use this answer to motivate yourself towards your financial goals.

Click Here To Check Out The Rest Of "Money: The Top 100 Best Ways To Make And Manage Money"

Check Out My Other Books

Below you'll find some of my other popular books and favorite products. Simply click on the pictures or links below to check them out and feel free to visit my website anytime at: www.AcesEbooks.com

Special Bonus: If you would like to get my latest **E-Books for FREE** just **CLICK HERE**

TOP 3 Peak Performance Products

Goals On Track

Hypnosis Downloads

Subliminal Power

Peak Performance Books

HABIT
The Top 100 Best Habits
How To Make A Positive Habit Permanent And How To Break Bad Habits
ACE McCLOUD

SELF DISCIPLINE
Unleash The Power Of Self Discipline, Influence And Willpower In Your Life To Achieve Anything
ACE McCLOUD

MOTIVATION
Master The Power Of Motivation To Propel Yourself To Success
ACE McCLOUD

CREATIVITY
Discover How To Unlock Your Creative Genius And Release The Power Within
ACE McCLOUD

Health Books

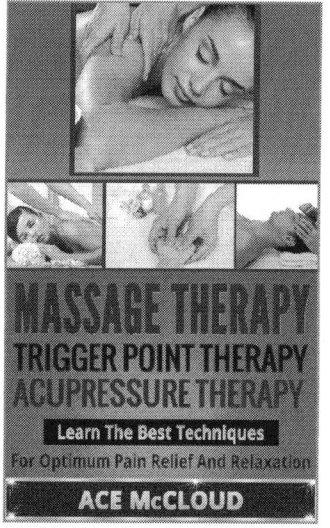

To See All My Book Click Here

Be sure to check out my website at: **www.AcesEbooks.com** for a complete list of all of my books and recommended products. I enjoy bringing you the best knowledge in the world and wish you the best in using this information to make your journey through life better and more enjoyable! **Best of luck to you!**

Ace's E-Books
The Best E-Books At The Best Price